A Collection of Fatherly Affirmations for Young Black Queens

Fearless Hearts

by Kenneth Braswell

Copyright © 2023 by Kenneth Braswell

All rights reserved. This book or any portion thereof may not be reproduced or used in any manner whatsoever without the express written permission of the publisher except for the use of brief quotations in a book review.

Printed in the United States of America
Publish Date: November 1, 2023
First Printing, 2023

979-8-9884899-9-3
(Hardcover)

Fathers Incorporated

2394 Mt. Vernon Road
STE 210
Dunwoody, GA 30338

www.fathersincorporated.com

NOTE FROM THE AUTHOR

Greetings, beautiful young queens,

I am Kenneth Braswell, the author of Fearless Hearts, and it is with immense pride and joy that I welcome you to this journey. This book is born out of decades of life experiences, lessons, triumphs, and mistakes, and it comes from a heart that beats with a fervent passion for uplifting and empowering the young black queens of tomorrow.

I am a father to four wonderful daughters, each one a queen in her own right. I've been blessed with the privilege of witnessing their growth, struggles, and victories, and it's been my honor to stand by their side as they've blossomed into powerful young women. But, the road has not always been smooth. There have been trials and errors, successes and failures, moments of certainty, and times of doubt.

Being a parent, particularly a father, to four daughters has taught me many valuable lessons. It has opened my eyes to the unique challenges faced by black girls in our society today and stirred in me a deep-seated desire to inspire, empower, and affirm each of them and all young black girls as they navigate their path to adulthood. That is what led me to write Fearless Hearts.

Fearless Hearts is more than just a journal. It's a love letter to my daughters, your daughters, and all young black girls across the globe. It's a tool, a guide, a beacon that I hope will light the way on your journey toward self-discovery, self-love, and empowerment.

As you delve into the chapters, engage with the narratives, ponder on the affirmations, and reflect on the reflection questions, my hope is that you will discover your strength, your voice, your worth, and the queen within you.

This journey will challenge you to recognize your unique beauty, your innate power, your boundless potential, and the innumerable ways in which you contribute to the richness and diversity of our world.

My ultimate hope is that, as you navigate through these pages, you will come to realize that you are more than enough just as you are. You are strong, you are smart, you are beautiful, and you are worthy. And, most importantly, you are loved.

Remember, your journey is not a race. It's a process of growth and learning, and every step, every challenge, every victory, and every setback is an integral part of your unique story. As you walk this path, I encourage you to do so fearlessly, with a heart full of courage, a mind full of ambition, and a soul full of resilience.

To the fearless hearts, the beautiful queens, welcome to this journey of self-discovery, empowerment, and growth. I am deeply honored to share this journey with you.

Onwards and upwards,
Kenneth Braswell

contents

13 — Introduction

- The Purpose of This Journal
- Understanding Affirmations: Their Power and Importance
- How to Use This Journal

23 — Chapter 1: Self-Love and Acceptance

- Recognizing Your Worth
- Celebrating Your Unique Features
- Embracing Your Authentic Hue: A Lesson from "Imitation of Life"
- Embracing Your Heritage
- Chapter Conclusion: Embrace Your Authentic Self

55 — Chapter 2: Confidence and Courage

- Understanding Confidence
- Standing Up for Yourself
- Angela Davis: A Beacon of Resilience and Advocacy
- Conquering Fear
- Fear Assessment for Young Black Queens
- Chapter Conclusion: The Power of Confidence and Courage

87 Chapter 3: Resilience and Perseverance

- Learning From Mistakes
- Handling Adversity
- Resilience Against Adversity: The Story of Dorothy Dandridge
- Overcoming Challenges
- Concluding the Chapter on Resilience and Perseverance

115 Chapter 4: Relationships and Communication

- Building Healthy Relationships
- Expressing Yourself Effectively
- Navigating Conflicts
- The Impact of Social Media on Socialization and Communication
- Chapter Conclusion: Relationships and Communication

137 Chapter 5: Ambition and Achievement

- Setting Goals
- Pursuing Dreams
- The Pursuit of Dreams: A Spotlight on Viola Davis
- Overcoming Obstacles to Success
- Chapter Conclusion: Ambition and Achievement
- Activity: The Challenge Bridge

163   Chapter 6: Body Image and Health

- Loving Your Body
- Prioritizing Health and Fitness
- Dealing with Body Changes and Puberty
- Daily Affirmations for Body Positivity

183   Chapter 7: Empowerment and Leadership

- Becoming a Leader
- Influencing Others Positively
- The Unstoppable Journey of Rihanna
- Empowering Others
- Daily Affirmations for Leadership

210   Conclusion

- Ongoing Journey: Continuing the Practice of Affirmations
- A Father's Hope: Closing Words from Contributors

> Each chapter begins with a brief introduction and discussion about the topic, followed by a collection of relevant affirmations. Each affirmation would have a small space for the reader to reflect on how the affirmation resonates with her or how she could apply it in her life. The intention is to make the journal interactive and engaging.

The Father's Dream: Richard Williams and His Champions

In the annals of sporting history, there are few stories as inspiring as that of Venus and Serena Williams. Behind their exceptional rise to the pinnacle of world tennis is a testament to the influence, dedication, and belief of a father in his daughters.

Richard Williams a man with a vision, whose audacious dreams for his daughters forever changed the landscape of tennis.

Raised in a poor neighborhood of Compton, California, Richard Williams had a vision of his daughters playing tennis long before they were even born.

Despite having little understanding of tennis himself, he learned the game and penned a 78-page plan to turn Venus and Serena into champions.

Not only did he dream of his daughters dominating the tennis courts, but he also aimed to use tennis as a tool to empower them and provide them with opportunities for a better life.

Richard began coaching Venus and Serena on the run-down tennis courts of Compton when they were only four and three years old.

Facing economic hardship, racial discrimination, and skepticism from the tennis community, Richard persevered, continuously instilling in his daughters the belief that they could overcome any obstacle and achieve their dreams.

His unwavering belief in his daughters' potential paid off. Venus and Serena Williams went on to become two of the greatest tennis players of all time, collectively winning dozens of Grand Slam titles and forever changing the face of a sport that had been traditionally dominated by white athletes.

But the story of Richard Williams and his daughters isn't the only example of a father's influence in shaping and empowering his daughters.

Take the story of Matthew Knowles, father to Beyoncé and Solange. Matthew helped guide Beyoncé's early career with Destiny's Child and continued to manage her solo career for several years. He was instrumental in helping Beyoncé become one of the most influential artists of her generation.

Similarly, Joe Jackson, despite his controversial methods, was a driving force behind the successful careers of his children, most notably his daughter Janet Jackson, who became a global pop icon.

These stories show the impact a father can have on his daughters' lives, helping them shape their opportunities, unlock their brilliance, encourage their power, and guide their purpose. They remind us that fathers, or father figures, have a crucial role in fostering an environment where their daughters feel supported and encouraged to chase their dreams and are instilled with the belief that no one can limit their potential.

So, my dear queens, know this - the support and encouragement of a father, or a father figure, can be an incredible source of strength. Whether it's your biological father, stepfather, grandfather, uncle, teacher, or mentor, these figures can help create an environment where you are free to dream, strive, and achieve without limitations.

> **Always remember that you are not just the architects of your dreams but also the builders of your destiny.**

Introduction: The Purpose of This Journal

Greetings, young queens!

Welcome to "Fearless Hearts: A Collection of Fatherly Affirmations for Young Black Queens." This special journal is written just for you as you navigate the exciting, challenging, and pivotal stage of middle school.

You are standing at the doorway to new experiences, ideas, and transformations, and we're here to assure you, you are more than ready for the journey ahead.

This is a book filled with strength, love, wisdom, and inspiration. It's drawn from the hearts of fathers who celebrate your unique power and beauty as a young black girl.

They understand the world you're growing in, the culture that enriches you, and the heritage that makes you who you are. These fathers know your potential and are rooting for your success.

> ✱ "Fearless Hearts" is designed as a guiding light, illuminating your path with affirmations that will help you believe in your abilities, build confidence, and inspire you to embrace your individuality. The affirmations in this book echo the wisdom and love that black fathers have imparted to their daughters for generations.

The eight chapters you will explore cover essential topics such as self-love, resilience, confidence, relationships, ambition, body image, and leadership. Each chapter begins with an introduction, followed by a series of affirmations and spaces for you to write your reflections.

These reflections are your personal interpretations, allowing you to internalize each affirmation and see how it can apply to your life. Why are affirmations so powerful?

- Affirmations are like seeds of positivity and self-belief.
- When you repeat them, internalize them, and act upon them, they can grow into strong trees of self-esteem, shaping how you view yourself and the world around you.

> And why from fathers? Fathers, or father figures, play an influential role in our lives. Their encouragement and support can be pillars of strength, building resilience, and fostering a sense of self-worth. These fatherly affirmations can empower you to navigate the world confidently, knowing you are loved, valued, and capable.

So, take your time with "Fearless Hearts." Absorb each affirmation. Reflect on it. Write about it. Let each word seep into your spirit, helping you recognize and affirm the brilliant, resilient, and beautiful queen that you are!

Now, are you ready to begin this journey of self-discovery and affirmation? Let's turn the page and start this empowering adventure together...

> You can't rely on how you look to sustain you. What is fundamentally beautiful is compassion for yourself and for those around you.
>
> - Lupita Nyong'o

Understanding Affirmations: Their Power and Importance

As you begin your journey with "Fearless Hearts," it's essential to understand what affirmations are and the significant role they can play in your life.

Affirmations are positive statements or declarations that help you challenge and overcome negative thoughts, doubts, and self-limiting beliefs. They are designed to encourage a positive and growth-focused mindset, one that can help you navigate through life's twists and turns with strength and grace.

> **Imagine affirmations as tiny seeds. When planted in your mind and heart and nourished with belief and repetition, these seeds can grow into mighty trees of confidence, resilience, and self-love. They have the power to shape your thoughts, which in turn shape your actions, habits, and, ultimately, your reality.**

Affirmations are particularly essential during your middle school years, a time when you're discovering more about yourself, your capabilities, and your place in the world. It's a period of change, growth, and sometimes, self-doubt.

 Amidst these fluctuating tides, affirmations can serve as anchors, providing stability, fostering self-belief, and reinforcing the knowledge that you have the strength to overcome any obstacle.

Let's break down the power of affirmations:

- **Shift in Mindset:** Affirmations can help replace negative thoughts with positive ones, shifting your mindset to focus on your strengths and possibilities rather than weaknesses and limitations.

- **Boost in Confidence:** Regularly affirming your abilities can help build and boost your self-confidence, enabling you to pursue your goals fearlessly.

- **Cultivation of Self-love:** Affirmations that emphasize your worth and uniqueness foster a sense of self-love and acceptance, essential elements for your overall well-being.

- **Promotion of Resilience:** Repeating affirmations can build mental resilience, helping you to remain positive and determined even in the face of challenges or setbacks.

- **Manifestation of Goals:** Affirmations can aid in the manifestation of your goals. By regularly affirming what you wish to achieve, you create a strong mental image that can guide your actions toward making it a reality.

- **Grounding and Centering:** In moments of stress or overwhelm, affirmations can help ground and center you, bringing you back to a place of calm and focus.

The affirmations in "Fearless Hearts" are designed to resonate deeply with you, to echo the love, strength, and wisdom that is part of your heritage as a young black queen. They acknowledge your unique journey and are here to remind you of the limitless potential within you.

> Remember, the real power of affirmations lies not just in reading them but in believing them and integrating them into your life.

As you navigate through this book, embrace these affirmations, repeat them, reflect on them, and most importantly, believe in them and in yourself.

> "I counted everything. I counted the steps to the road, the steps up to the church, the number of dishes and silverware I washed anything that could be counted, I did."

- Katherine Johnson

How to Use This Journal

"Fearless Hearts: A Collection of Fatherly Affirmations for Young Black Queens" is designed to be your personal companion, guiding light, and self-empowerment tool.

Here are some suggestions on how you can get the most out of this journal:

1. **Read Regularly:** Try to read the affirmations in this journal daily, if you can. Consistency is key when it comes to using affirmations. Regular exposure to positive statements can help reinforce these messages in your mind, encouraging a more positive and empowered mindset.

2. **Reflect on Each Affirmation:** After reading each affirmation, take a moment to reflect. What does the affirmation mean to you? How does it apply to your life? Use the spaces provided to write down your thoughts and feelings. This process can help you internalize each affirmation.

3. **Speak It:** Affirmations are most powerful when spoken out loud. Read the affirmations aloud to yourself, say them in front of a mirror, or record yourself saying them. The act of hearing these positive affirmations can reinforce their message and help to boost your self-confidence and self-belief further.

4. **Visualize:** As you recite an affirmation, visualize it as already being true. This can help to strengthen the positive impact of the affirmation on your subconscious mind.

5. **Personalize:** Feel free to adapt the affirmations if you need to. Make them personal to you. The more an affirmation resonates with you, the more powerful it will be.

6. **Be Patient:** Remember, change doesn't happen overnight. Be patient with yourself. The power of affirmations lies in their repetition over time. Keep at it and have faith in the process.

7. **Stay Open-Minded:** Some affirmations may seem more relevant to you than others, and that's okay. Stay open to each message, you might be surprised by what resonates with you over time.

8. **Create a Routine:** Incorporate the practice of reading and reflecting on affirmations into your daily routine. It could be part of your morning wake-up ritual, an evening wind-down practice, or a self-care break during your day.

Remember, "Fearless Hearts" is a journey, not a destination. There's no rush to get through it.

The goal is not to finish the book quickly but to let each affirmation seep into your heart and mind, fostering a deep-seated sense of self-belief, strength, and self-love. Enjoy the journey, young queens!

Part: 1

Self-Love and Acceptance

> "You alone are enough. You have nothing to prove to anybody."
>
> - Maya Angelou

Self-Love and Acceptance

Welcome to the first step on your journey of self-discovery and affirmation - self-love and acceptance.

This foundational chapter aims to ignite the flame of self-appreciation within you and encourage you to embrace the entirety of who you are, inside and out.

As a young black queen, it's essential to understand that your unique attributes - your mind, your heart, your spirit, your heritage, your complexion, your hair, your body - all contribute to your distinct beauty and strength.

> **Recognizing, accepting, and loving these aspects of yourself is the essence of self-love. When you love and accept yourself just as you are, you set the stage for growth, confidence, and resilience to navigate life's challenges.**

The affirmations in this chapter are woven with words of love, encouragement, and appreciation.

- They aim to reflect back to you the beauty, strength, and worth that lies within you.
- They are here to remind you that you are enough, just as you are.

Affirmations:

1. "I am a unique, beautiful, and powerful expression of life."
2. "I love and accept myself, just as I am."
3. "I am worthy of love, respect, and kindness."
4. "I celebrate the skin I am in - it is the shade of strength and beauty."
5. "I honor and value my heritage as a source of pride and strength."

 Embrace these affirmations, repeat them, and believe in them. Most importantly, use them to nourish the seeds of self-love and acceptance within your heart.

Remember, you are a queen, deserving of all the love and respect in the world, starting with the love and respect you give yourself.

This is your space to write, draw, doodle, or sketch your ideas and plans!

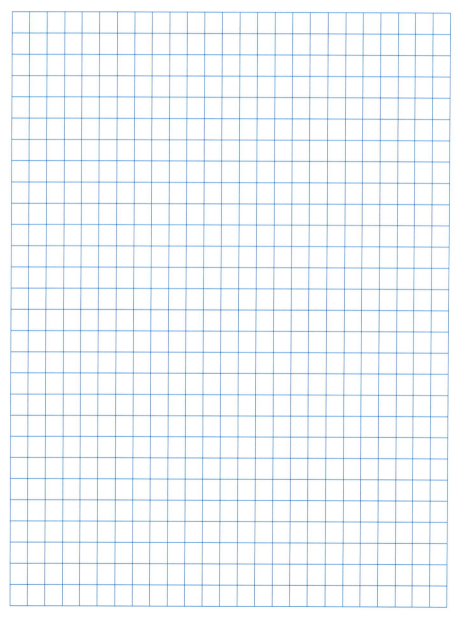

Key Takeaways:

1. **Self-love is Empowering:** When you love and accept yourself, you affirm your worth and strengthen your belief in your abilities. This is an empowering state of being that can influence all aspects of your life.

2. **Unconditional Acceptance:** Self-love means accepting yourself unconditionally and acknowledging your strengths and areas for growth. This acceptance is not based on conditions, achievements, or validations from others.

3. **Foundation for Growth:** Self-love and acceptance create a positive environment for personal growth. When you love yourself, you're more likely to invest time and energy into your growth and development.

4. **Rejection of Negative Stereotypes:** Embracing self-love allows you to reject negative stereotypes and societal pressures that can impact your self-esteem. It empowers you to define your own worth.

5. **Protection Against Negative Influences:** Strong self-love can serve as a shield against negative influences. When you truly value yourself, you're less likely to let others' negative opinions impact you.

6. **Starting Point for Healthy Relationships:** Self-love sets the standard for how you expect to be treated by others. It's the foundation for developing healthy, respectful relationships.

Recognizing Your Worth

Recognizing your worth is an integral part of self-love and acceptance. It's about understanding and appreciating your intrinsic value, that you are important and valuable, just as you are.

Your worth is not determined by external factors like achievements, physical appearance, or what others think of you.

Rather, it's rooted in your existence, your unique qualities, and the potential within you.

> **As a young black queen, you carry within you a rich legacy of strength, resilience, wisdom, and beauty. Your worth is as vast as the heritage you carry and the dreams that flutter in your heart.**

Knowing this, and embracing this, can provide a foundation of self-esteem and confidence that can carry you through life's ups and downs.

Affirmations:

Here are three affirmations to help you recognize and affirm your worth:

1. "I am worthy of love, success, and happiness."
2. "My worth is not defined by others' opinions, but by my true essence and potential."
3. "I honor and cherish my worth, as priceless as a queen's crown."

Reflective Questions:

As you ponder these affirmations, reflect on these questions in your journal:

1. What qualities or characteristics do you believe make you valuable? Think beyond external qualities to traits like your kindness, creativity, determination, or resilience.
2. How does it feel to affirm your worth through the affirmations above? Do you find it easy, challenging, or somewhere in between? Reflect on why that might be.
3. What are some ways you can honor and affirm your worth on a daily basis? This could be anything from saying positive affirmations to standing up for yourself, to spending time doing something you love.

> **Recognizing your worth is a journey, one that you'll continue to navigate as you grow. Remember, young queen, your worth is immense, unchanging, and is your birthright. Hold onto this truth, and let it guide you through your middle school years and beyond.**

This is your space to write, draw, doodle, or sketch your ideas and plans!

Celebrating Your Unique Features

Each one of us is unique, carrying a blend of features that make us who we are. Our features go beyond our physical attributes to include our skills, talents, interests, and even the way we think or perceive the world.

❋ These features, when acknowledged and celebrated, can form a solid foundation of self-love and acceptance.

As a young black queen, your unique features may include your resilient spirit, your radiant melanin skin, your versatile and expressive hair, your heritage, your values, and the dreams that you hold in your heart.

All these characteristics and more come together to create the masterpiece that is you.

> Celebrating your unique features means recognizing them, embracing them, and being proud of them. It means respecting your individuality and understanding that you are perfect in your uniqueness.

Affirmations:

Here are three affirmations that celebrate your unique features:

1. "I am proud of who I am, and I celebrate my unique features."

2. "My features are a testament to my strength, heritage, and individuality."

3. "I am a masterpiece, beautifully crafted in my uniqueness."

Reflective Questions:

Reflect on these affirmations and journal your thoughts with these guiding questions:

1. What are some unique features that you love about yourself? This could be physical characteristics, talents, skills, or even personal values.

2. How do these unique features contribute to your sense of self? How do they shape your identity and self-perception?

3. How can you celebrate your unique features more in your daily life? Consider actions that highlight these features or express gratitude for them.

Celebrating your unique features is not about vanity or arrogance. It's about self-acknowledgment and appreciation. It's about understanding that your unique features make you the beautiful, powerful, and capable young queen that you are. Keep celebrating, keep shining, and remember - there is no one else in the world quite like you.

This is your space to write, draw, doodle, or sketch your ideas and plans!

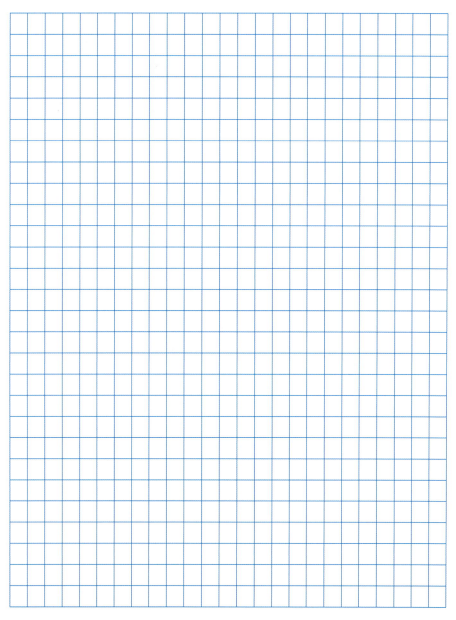

EMBRACING YOUR AUTHENTIC HUE: A LESSON FROM "IMITATION OF LIFE"

"Imitation of Life," a classic film with timeless messages, provides a poignant backdrop for an essential truth: Every individual, irrespective of their skin color, is unique, beautiful, and worthy.

The movie unfolds the stories of two women, one white and one black, and their daughters. Their intertwined lives bring forth significant themes around identity, acceptance, and self-love.

> The most impactful narrative for our discussion here is that of Sarah Jane, the light-skinned daughter of Annie, the black housekeeper. Struggling with her identity in a racially divided society, Sarah Jane decides to pass as white, rejecting her mother and her African American heritage.

Sarah Jane's story serves as a stark reminder of the damaging effects of societal pressures and stereotypes, where people feel compelled to deny their authentic selves to fit into pre-set molds.

This narrative also underlines the vital importance of self-love and acceptance, especially when it comes to one's racial identity.

As a young black queen, the message to take from Sarah Jane's story is not one of sorrow but rather a call to stand in your truth and celebrate your identity.

Remember that your skin color, your features, your heritage - they are not merely characteristics; they form an integral part of who you are. They are the threads in the vibrant tapestry that is your identity, and each one adds to your uniqueness, your beauty, and your worth.

AFFIRMATIONS:

Let's recite these affirmations inspired by "Imitation of Life":

1. "I embrace and celebrate my skin color as part of my unique beauty."
2. "I am worthy and valuable, exactly as I am."
3. "I stand proud in my truth, honoring my heritage and identity."

REFLECTIVE QUESTIONS:

As you reflect on these affirmations, consider these questions:

1. How did you feel about Sarah Jane's choice in "Imitation of Life"? Can you empathize with her struggles, even as you understand the importance of staying true to yourself?
2. What does your skin color represent to you? Consider its historical, cultural, and personal significance.
3. How can you celebrate your skin color and use it as a source of strength and pride in your daily life?

In a world that often tries to fit us into boxes, standing in your truth can be a radical act of self-love. Your skin color, your unique features, your heritage - these are the beautiful melodies in the symphony of who you are.

Like Sarah Jane, you may encounter societal pressures, but unlike her, you have the power to embrace your authentic self, affirming that you are unique, beautiful, and worthy in your own right.

This is your space to write, draw, doodle, or sketch your ideas and plans!

Embracing Your Heritage

Our heritage is like a river, a continuous flow of cultural traditions, values, and histories passed down through generations. It shapes our identity, influencing our beliefs, behaviors, and sense of belonging.

> **Embracing your heritage means acknowledging this vital stream of life, appreciating its richness, and understanding the valuable lessons it imparts.**

As a young black queen, your heritage holds immense power and beauty. It tells the story of resilient ancestors, groundbreaking achievements, deep-rooted traditions, and transformative movements. It sings the songs of strength, wisdom, courage, and perseverance.

By embracing your heritage, you honor this narrative, allowing it to empower your journey and inspire your dreams.

Affirmations:

Here are three affirmations that highlight the power of embracing your heritage:

1. "I am a proud carrier of a rich heritage that strengthens and defines me."
2. "My heritage is a powerful testament to resilience, strength, and beauty."
3. "I honor my roots as they ground me and guide my growth."

Reflective Questions:

Reflect on these affirmations and journal your responses to these guiding questions:

1. What does your heritage mean to you? How does it shape your identity, beliefs, and behaviors?
2. What aspects of your heritage are you most proud of and why? Consider traditions, historical events, cultural practices, or values that resonate with you.
3. How can you actively honor and celebrate your heritage in your daily life? This could be through learning more about your history, practicing cultural traditions, or sharing stories with friends and family.

Remember, embracing your heritage is not just about looking back. It's also about carrying the legacy forward, weaving your own chapters into the story. Your heritage is a beacon, illuminating your past, enriching your present, and guiding your future.

As a young black queen, your heritage is a crown that you wear with pride, affirming the strength, beauty, and power that flows within you.

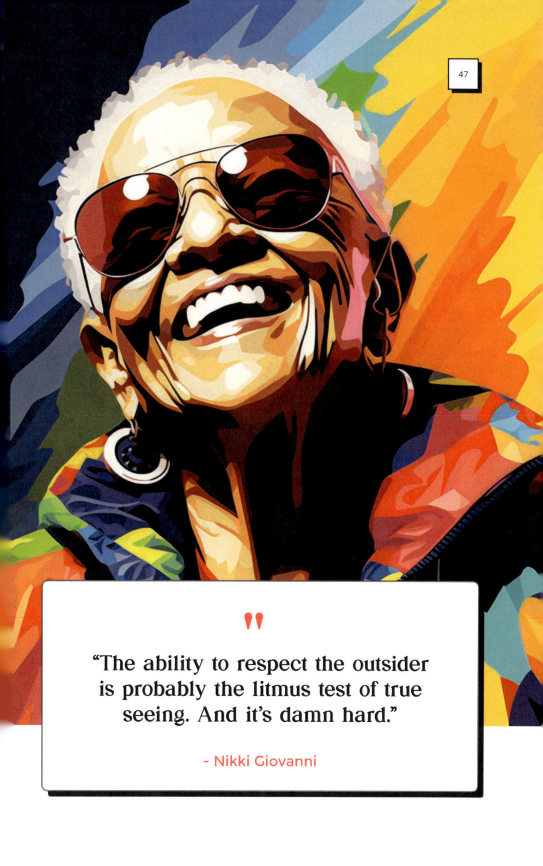

> "The ability to respect the outsider is probably the litmus test of true seeing. And it's damn hard."
>
> - Nikki Giovanni

This is your space to write, draw, doodle, or sketch your ideas and plans!

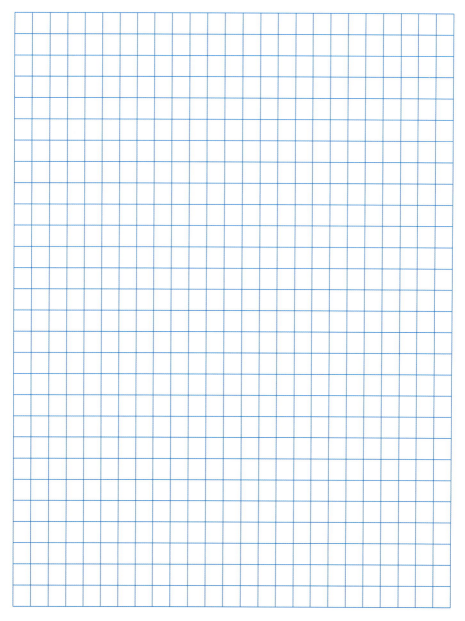

Chapter Conclusion: Embrace Your Authentic Self

As we conclude this transformative chapter, let's revisit the essence of our journey - self-love, acceptance, recognizing your worth, celebrating your unique features, and embracing your heritage.

> These facets come together to paint a holistic picture of who you are - a young black queen, radiant in her authenticity and powerful in her truth.

Remember, dear queen, that your journey towards self-love and acceptance is just that - a journey. There may be days when you stumble or falter, and that's okay. It's all part of growing, learning, and becoming the best version of yourself.

Affirmations are like seeds; when sown into the garden of your mind and nurtured with belief and repetition, they can bloom into beautiful flowers of self-love and acceptance. They are words of power, helping you to shape your mindset and beliefs, paving the way towards a fulfilling, confident life.

> In the words of the phenomenal Maya Angelou, "You alone are enough. You have nothing to prove to anybody." Carry these words in your heart as an affirmation of your worth and value.

💬 And, as the admirable Oprah Winfrey once said, "The more you praise and celebrate your life, the more there is in life to celebrate."

Let this quote inspire you to continuously celebrate your unique features and the vibrant heritage that contributes to your unique identity.

❗❗ Finally, remember the words of Ralph Waldo Emerson, "To be yourself in a world that is constantly trying to make you something else is the greatest accomplishment."

> **You, young queen, have the power to make a difference, starting with loving and accepting yourself, recognizing your worth, and celebrating your heritage.**

This chapter was just the beginning, a step towards a journey filled with self-love, acceptance, and empowerment. Keep these affirmations close to your heart, reflect on them, and watch as they transform your life, one day at a time.

❋ Remember, you are a queen - unique, beautiful, and worthy of every great thing that life has to offer.

> "The success of every woman should be the inspiration to another. We should raise each other up."
>
> - Serena Williams

Chapter: 2

Confidence and Courage

"I love myself. The quietest. Simplest. Most powerful. Revolution. Ever."

- Nayyirah Waheed

Confidence and Courage

Our journey towards self-love and acceptance opens the door to two empowering allies: confidence and courage. Confidence illuminates our abilities and self-belief, while courage empowers us to face challenges, take risks, and step into our true potential.

Together, they provide a foundation for personal growth and success.

> As a young black queen, confidence and courage can be transformative tools. When wielded with wisdom, they can help you navigate the rough seas of middle school, the riddles of adolescence, and beyond.

They can help you stand tall in your truth, follow your dreams, and create a future that resonates with your values and aspirations.

 In this chapter, we will explore these two pillars of personal power. We will delve into the realm of self-belief, assertiveness, resilience, and bravery.

Through narratives, affirmations, and reflections, we aim to awaken the confident, courageous queen within you.

Affirmations:

Here are three affirmations to set the tone for this chapter:

1. "I am confident in my abilities and courageous in my actions."
2. "I face challenges with courage and emerge stronger."
3. "I confidently express my thoughts and feelings, standing in my truth."

Key Takeaways:

As we journey through this chapter, we aim to achieve the following key takeaways:

1. **Understand Confidence:** You'll gain a deeper understanding of confidence, its importance, and ways to nurture it. You'll explore the connection between self-love and confidence and learn how to cultivate self-belief.

2. **Discover Courage:** We'll delve into the concept of courage, including its role in overcoming fears, handling setbacks, and taking healthy risks. We'll explore stories of courage and resilience from inspiring black women.

3. **Confidence and Courage in Action:** We'll explore practical ways to apply confidence and courage in daily life. This includes dealing with peer pressure, handling academic challenges, and standing up for what's right.

❞ Remember, young queen, in the words of Beyoncé, "The most alluring thing a woman can have is confidence." And as Rosa Parks said, "I have learned over the years that when one's mind is made up, this diminishes fear; knowing what must be done does away with fear."

Let these affirmations and quotes guide you as we delve into the empowering world of confidence and courage. Embrace this journey, for it is a stepping stone to unlocking the fearless and confident queen within you.

> "You may not always have a comfortable life, and you will not always be able to solve all of the world's problems at once but don't ever underestimate the importance you can have because history has shown us that courage can be contagious and hope can take on a life of its own."

- First Lady Michelle Obama

Understanding Confidence

Confidence is a beacon of self-assurance that guides you through life. It is the belief in your abilities, the conviction that you are capable of accomplishing your goals, and the strength to express your thoughts and feelings without fear.

> **Confidence is not about being perfect or the best; it is about acknowledging your worth, appreciating your strengths, and embracing your potential.**

As a young black queen, cultivating confidence is crucial. It empowers you to take charge of your life, step outside your comfort zone, and strive towards your dreams.

* Confidence also helps you navigate challenging situations, making your voice heard, and standing tall in your authenticity.

Affirmations:

Here are three affirmations to help nurture your confidence:

1. "I am capable and confident in my abilities to achieve my goals."
2. "I trust in my strength and express my thoughts and feelings with confidence."
3. "I am worthy of respect and treat myself and others with kindness and understanding."

Reflective Questions:

Reflect on these affirmations and consider these guiding questions:

1. What does confidence mean to you? How do you define it, and what role does it play in your life?
2. What are your strengths? How can you use these strengths to build your confidence?
3. Can you recall a time when you felt confident? What did you learn from that experience, and how can you carry that feeling into other areas of your life?

❋ Remember, confidence is not a destination but a journey. It's not something that you either have or don't have. Instead, it's a quality that you can nurture and grow over time.

❗❗ As the remarkable Serena Williams once said, "The success of every woman should be the inspiration to another. We should raise each other up."

Let this inspire you to not only build your confidence but to help lift others too. You are a young black queen, and within you lies a wellspring of untapped confidence, ready to rise.

This is your space to write, draw, doodle, or sketch your ideas and plans!

Standing Up for Yourself

To stand up for yourself is to claim your space in the world, asserting your worth, your rights, and your voice. It is about advocating for your needs and boundaries and refusing to be treated less than you deserve.

* When you stand up for yourself, you demonstrate self-respect and confidence, empowering yourself and inspiring others.

As a young black queen, standing up for yourself is an act of power. It's a testament to your strength, courage, and integrity.

> It shows the world—and yourself—that you value your well-being and are willing to protect it.

Affirmations:

Here are three affirmations to reinforce this important skill:

1. "I respect myself and insist upon it from everybody else."
2. "I have the courage to express my feelings and stand up for my beliefs."
3. "I set healthy boundaries and take care of my emotional well-being."

Reflective Questions:

Reflect on these affirmations and respond to the following questions:

1. What does it mean to you to stand up for yourself? How does it align with your understanding of respect and self-worth?
2. Can you recall a time when you stood up for yourself? How did it feel, and what was the outcome?
3. What are some situations where you find it difficult to stand up for yourself? What strategies can you use to assert yourself in these situations?

Remember, standing up for yourself doesn't mean being combative or disrespectful. It's about communicating your feelings and needs assertively and respectfully.

❗❗ In the wise words of Maya Angelou, "Never make someone a priority when all you are to them is an option." You are worthy of respect and kindness, both from others and from yourself.

As a young black queen, standing up for yourself is a powerful affirmation of your self-worth and confidence.

This is your space to write, draw, doodle, or sketch your ideas and plans!

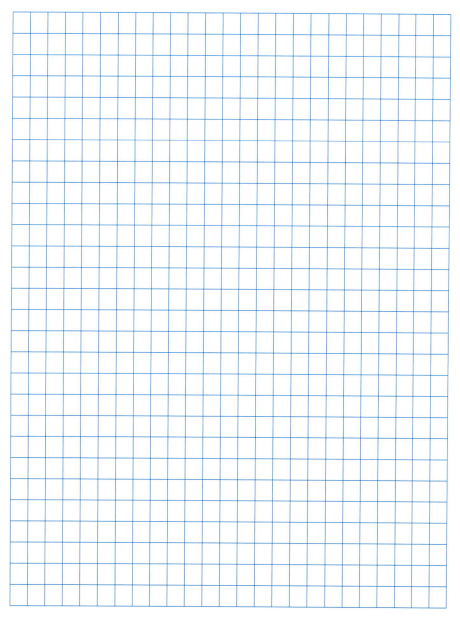

Angela Davis:
A Beacon of Resilience and Advocacy

Angela Davis is an iconic figure whose story illuminates the power of resilience, courage, and standing up for what you believe is right. Born in 1944 in Birmingham, Alabama, she grew up in a society marked by racial segregation and social injustices.

> **Rather than succumb to these oppressions, Angela chose to stand tall, transforming her lived experiences into fuel for a lifelong commitment to social activism.**

As a young scholar, Angela was deeply moved by the philosophy of social and political change. She explored ideologies that championed equality, social justice, and liberation, equipping her with the knowledge that would later shape her activism.

Angela understood the power of education as a tool for liberation, a belief that guided her journey as a student, a teacher, and a lifelong learner.

* In the late 1960s and early 1970s, Angela emerged as a prominent leader in the Civil Rights Movement and the Communist Party USA. She championed the rights of the marginalized, fought against racial and economic injustices, and advocated for prison reform.

Angela wasn't just standing up for herself; she was standing up for her community and for the ideals of justice and equality.

Her advocacy didn't come without a cost. In 1970, she was accused of murder, kidnapping, and conspiracy due to her involvement in a violent courthouse incident.

She spent roughly a year in jail before her trial. During this time, a global movement formed advocating for her release, led by the rallying cry, "Free Angela Davis!"

Angela was eventually acquitted of all charges in 1972, a testament to her resilience and the power of collective action.

> Today, Angela Davis continues to teach, write, and advocate for social justice. Her story is a shining example of standing up for one's beliefs, regardless of the circumstances.

It conveys the message that we all have a voice and the power to use it to not only stand up for others but also for ourselves.

Reflective Questions:

Reflect on Angela's story and consider these questions:

1. What aspects of Angela Davis's story inspire you? What can you learn from her courage, resilience, and commitment to standing up for her beliefs?

2. How does Angela's story influence your understanding of using your voice and standing up for yourself?

3. In what ways can you use your voice to stand up for your beliefs and advocate for yourself and others in your life?

❗❗ Remember, in the words of Angela Davis herself, "You have to act as if it were possible to radically transform the world. And you have to do it all the time."

As a young black queen, your voice matters, and your courage can make a difference. Like Angela, you can rise above challenges, stand tall in your truth, and effect meaningful change.

This is your space to write, draw, doodle, or sketch your ideas and plans!

Conquering Fear

Fear is a universal emotion that we all experience. It can make our hearts race, our palms sweat, and our minds swirl with worry.

But fear can also be a powerful motivator, a signal that we are about to step out of our comfort zone, grow, and transform.

> **As a young black queen, you will undoubtedly face fears. But remember this: fear does not define you. It does not determine your capabilities or your worth. Instead, fear can serve as a stepping stone, a challenge to conquer and transform into courage.**

AFFIRMATIONS:

Here are three affirmations to help you conquer your fears:

1. "I face my fears with courage and turn them into opportunities for growth."
2. "I am stronger than my fears; they do not control me."
3. "Every step I take in spite of fear reaffirms my courage and strength."

REFLECTIVE QUESTIONS:

Reflect on these affirmations and consider these reflection questions:

1. What fears do you currently have? How do these fears affect your daily life and decisions?
2. Can you recall a time when you faced a fear and overcame it? What did you learn from that experience, and how did it shape your view of fear?
3. How can you use your fears as motivation to grow and step out of your comfort zone? What strategies can you implement to conquer your fears?

Remember, fear is natural and part of the human experience. It's not about eliminating fear completely, but learning to manage it, to stand up to it, and to continue moving forward despite it.

❗❗ As the incredible First Lady, Michelle Obama once said, "Don't ever make decisions based on fear. Make decisions based on hope and possibility."

As a young black queen, you have the power within you to conquer your fears and let your courage shine brightly.

This is your space to write, draw, doodle, or sketch your ideas and plans!

Fear Assessment Tool for Young Black Queens

This assessment is designed to help you identify any fears you may be experiencing. Please remember this is a self-assessment tool and should not replace professional help.

> If your fears are impacting your day-to-day life, please seek assistance from a trusted adult or a mental health professional.

Instructions:

On a scale from 1 (never) to 5 (always), rate the following statements based on how often you feel this way.

- ☐ I avoid certain situations because they scare me.
- ☐ I worry about what others think of me.
- ☐ I feel anxious about making mistakes or failing.
- ☐ I am scared of speaking up or voicing my opinions.
- ☐ I feel afraid of the future or the unknown.
- ☐ I am worried about fitting in or being accepted by my peers.
- ☐ I feel scared about standing up for myself.
- ☐ I am afraid of taking on new challenges or trying new things.
- ☐ I worry about my performance at school.
- ☐ I fear being judged for being myself.

Scoring:

- **10-20: Low Fear Level** – You seem to manage your fears effectively. Continue using your coping strategies and maintaining your confidence. Remember, it's okay to ask for help if new fears arise or if existing ones become more challenging.

- **21-35: Moderate Fear Level** – You experience some fears that may occasionally hold you back. Consider techniques for managing fear, like deep breathing, visualization, or talking to someone you trust about your fears. You might also find it helpful to seek guidance from a trusted adult or a counselor.

- **36-50: High Fear Level** – Your fears seem to be significantly affecting your life. It's essential to talk to someone about these feelings. Reach out to a trusted adult, like a parent, teacher, or school counselor. They can provide support and possibly refer you to a mental health professional who can help you navigate and overcome your fears.

Results:

Regardless of your score, remember that experiencing fear is a natural part of life. However, if your fears are holding you back, it's important to seek help.

As a young black queen, remember that fear does not define you. You possess the courage to face and conquer your fears, and there are many resources available to help you do so.

Chapter Conclusion: The Power of Confidence and Courage

As we close this chapter on Confidence and Courage, remember, dear young black queens, you are at the heart of this journey.

This chapter was meant to inspire and equip you to face your fears, to voice your beliefs, and to believe in your infinite worth.
In the spirit of confidence and courage, let's reflect on some powerful affirmations and quotes from influential black women:

> "I love myself. The quietest. Simplest. Most powerful. Revolution. Ever." - Nayyirah Waheed.

Loving yourself is the foundation of confidence. Remember, you are worthy of love, especially from yourself.

> "I will not have my life narrowed down. I will not bow down to somebody else's whim or to someone else's ignorance." - Bell Hooks.

Always stand up for yourself and your beliefs. Don't let anyone dim your light or belittle your worth.

> "Don't wait around for other people to be happy for you. Any happiness you get, you've got to make yourself." - Alice Walker.

This emphasizes the courage it takes to seek your own happiness, independent of others' opinions or validation.

Remember, confidence and courage are like muscles; the more you use them, the stronger they get.

Take comfort in knowing it's okay to be afraid or unsure - even the most influential black women have experienced these feelings.

> What's most important is that you face your fears, stand up for what you believe in, and hold on to your self-belief.

You are a young black queen full of potential, power, and promise. Keep learning, growing, and striving. In your journey towards becoming a courageous and confident young woman, remember to celebrate each step forward, no matter how small.

> As we end this chapter, think of the words of Maya Angelou, "I can be changed by what happens to me. But I refuse to be reduced by it."

Carry this mantra with you, and let it empower you to face each day with courage and confidence. You are more than capable, dear queens. You are strength embodied.

> Reflect on these words as you navigate the exciting, challenging, and transformative middle school years. It's a journey filled with growth and discovery.

CHAPTER: 3

Resilience and Perseverance

> "Each person must live their life as a model for others."
>
> - Rosa Parks

Resilience and Perseverance

Welcome to Chapter 3, dear young black queens. In this chapter, we explore two powerful attributes that will aid your journey through life – resilience and perseverance.

Just like confidence and courage, these are not qualities you are simply born with; they are skills you cultivate and develop as you face and overcome life's challenges.

> **Resilience is the ability to bounce back from difficulties or setbacks. It's the inner strength that helps you to weather the storms of life and come out on the other side stronger and wiser.**

Perseverance, on the other hand, is the unwavering determination to keep going, to keep striving, no matter how tough the journey might be.

These qualities are essential for every young black queen. You'll face challenges - that's a part of life - but how you respond to these challenges is what truly matters.

> 🗣️ "Forgive yourself for your faults and your mistakes and move on."- Les Brown

This chapter will guide you in understanding the importance of resilience and perseverance and equip you with affirmations to cultivate these qualities.

> You'll also encounter stories of influential black women who have demonstrated incredible resilience and perseverance.

Key Takeaways:

1. **Understanding the importance of resilience and perseverance:** Recognize how these qualities empower you to navigate life's challenges and become stronger.

2. **Developing resilience and perseverance through affirmations and reflection:** Learn powerful affirmations to cultivate resilience and perseverance, and engage in reflection exercises to strengthen these qualities.

3. **Drawing inspiration from influential black women:** Be inspired by stories of incredible black women who have demonstrated extraordinary resilience and perseverance in their lives.

Remember, the journey to building resilience and perseverance is a process, not a destination. It's about learning, growing, and becoming the best version of yourself.

As you navigate through this chapter, know that every challenge is an opportunity for growth, and every setback is a setup for a comeback.

> As the great Sojourner Truth once said: "Truth is powerful and it prevails." Keep this in mind as you explore the power of resilience and perseverance.

Learning From Mistakes

Mistakes. We all make them. But the most crucial thing to remember is that mistakes are not failures; they are opportunities for learning and growth.

Making a mistake does not decrease your worth, nor does it define who you are. It merely signifies that you're trying, exploring, and stepping out of your comfort zone.

> Being a young black queen, you're embarking on a journey full of discovery and sometimes, that means stumbling. But remember, every stumble, every fall, teaches us something important about ourselves and the world around us.

Affirmations:

Here are three affirmations to help you embrace the learning that comes from making mistakes:

1. "Every mistake I make is a step forward in my journey of growth."
2. "I am not defined by my mistakes, but by how I learn and grow from them."
3. "I embrace my mistakes as opportunities to become stronger and wiser."

Reflective Questions:

Now, let's reflect on these affirmations with the following questions:

1. Can you recall a recent mistake you made? How did you feel about it, and what did you learn from it?
2. How can you change your perspective to view mistakes as opportunities for growth rather than failures?
3. How can the affirmations above help you cope with future mistakes?

✱ Remember, it's natural to feel disappointed when we make mistakes, but it's also important to recognize the power they have to propel us forward in our growth.

❝ As the phenomenal Maya Angelou said, "We may encounter many defeats, but we must not be defeated. It may even be necessary to encounter the defeat, so that we can know who we are. So that we can see, oh, that happened, and I rose. I did get knocked down flat in front of the whole world, and I rose."

So, dear young queens, take comfort in your journey, embrace your mistakes, and use them as stepping stones on your path to growth and self-discovery.

> **Remember, your mistakes are proof that you are trying, and trying is a testament to your resilience and perseverance.**

This is your space to write, draw, doodle, or sketch your ideas and plans!

Handling Adversity

> **Life's journey isn't always smooth sailing. There will be times of calm and times of storm, and it's during these stormy periods – when we face adversity – that we get the chance to truly grow.**

It might be tough, and you may feel overwhelmed, but remember, as a young black queen, you carry within you the strength and wisdom of generations.

Facing adversity is not about avoiding the storm but learning how to dance in the rain. It's about resilience, perseverance, and drawing on your inner strength to overcome the hurdles that come your way.

Affirmations:

Here are three affirmations to empower you when facing adversity:

1. "I am stronger than any challenge that comes my way."

2. "Adversity is not a roadblock but a stepping stone to my growth."

3. "I hold the power to transform challenges into opportunities."

Reflective Questions:

Now, let's take a moment to reflect on these affirmations:

1. Think of a time when you faced adversity. How did you react? What did you learn about yourself in the process?

2. How can the above affirmations help you face future adversities? Do they alter your perspective on challenges and setbacks?

3. Is there an influential black woman who inspires you with her resilience in the face of adversity? What specific actions or attitudes can you adopt from her?

❝ As you consider these questions, remember the words of Serena Williams, a top-notch athlete who faced many adversities: "Every woman's success should be an inspiration to another. We're strongest when we cheer each other on."

So, my dear queens, embrace adversity as part of your journey. It's not there to break you but to shape you, to transform you into the strong, resilient, and phenomenal black woman you are destined to be.

> **Adversity isn't a sign of failure; it's a testament to your strength. Stand tall, stay strong, and keep moving forward.**

This is your space to write, draw, doodle, or sketch your ideas and plans!

Resilience Against Adversity: The Story of Dorothy Dandridge

There are many powerful examples of black women who have demonstrated incredible resilience and perseverance in the face of adversity.

One such woman is Dorothy Dandridge, a renowned singer and actress whose tale is a testament to the power of never allowing anyone to limit your opportunities, brilliance, or purpose.

Dorothy Dandridge was a trailblazer in every sense of the word. Born in 1922, she rose to fame during a time when black women were largely marginalized and discriminated against, particularly in the entertainment industry.

> Despite the adversities of racism and prejudice, Dandridge refused to let societal biases limit her abilities or dreams. As a singer, she charmed audiences with her powerful voice and captivating stage presence.
>
> However, her path was anything but easy. She faced blatant racism, often performing in venues where she, because of her skin color, was not allowed to dine or stay.

But Dandridge, ever the fighter, didn't let these adversities dampen her spirit. Instead, they fueled her determination to break down the barriers of discrimination.

She stood her ground and, through her undeniable talent and unwavering resilience, Dandridge became the first African American woman to be nominated for an Academy Award for Best Actress, forever changing the course of Hollywood.

Her journey was not without its challenges, but her story serves as a powerful reminder: never allow anyone or anything to limit your opportunities, your brilliance, your power, your purpose, your desires, or your goals.

Affirmations:

As you reflect on Dandridge's story, consider these affirmations:

1. "Just like Dorothy Dandridge, I am limitless in my potential."
2. "No person or circumstance can dim my brilliance or power."
3. "I am resilient, and I will rise above adversity."

❋ Think about this incredible woman's journey and her refusal to be limited by adversity. Take inspiration from her resilience and use it to fuel your own journey, dear young queens.

> Remember, the only limitations you have are the ones you accept. Stand strong, keep striving, and let your brilliance shine, just like Dorothy Dandridge did.

This is your space to write, draw, doodle, or sketch your ideas and plans!

Overcoming Challenges

Just as a diamond is formed under pressure, so too are we shaped by the challenges we face. Challenges can be tough, they can push us, test us, and sometimes even make us question our abilities.

> **But remember, young black queens, each challenge you face is an opportunity to grow, to learn, and to emerge stronger.**

When faced with a challenge, it's natural to feel a bit overwhelmed or even scared. But it's important to remember that these feelings don't define you.

* You are defined by your ability to rise above these challenges, to learn from them, and to use them as stepping stones to reach your full potential.

AFFIRMATIONS:

Here are three affirmations to remind you of your inherent ability to overcome challenges:

1. "I am capable of overcoming any challenges that come my way."
2. "Challenges are opportunities for me to grow and learn."
3. "I embrace challenges because they make me stronger."

REFLECTIVE QUESTIONS:

Reflect on these affirmations with the following questions:

1. Can you recall a time when you overcame a challenge? How did it feel, and what did you learn from the experience?
2. How can you use the above affirmations to change your perspective on future challenges?
3. Think of a black woman who inspires you with her ability to overcome challenges. What can you learn from her journey?

❢❢ Remember the words of the influential black scholar and cultural anthropologist Zora Neale Hurston, "I have the nerve to walk my own way, however hard, in my search for reality, rather than climb upon the rattling wagon of wishful illusions."

So, my dear young queens, know that challenges will come, but you are more than capable of overcoming them.

❋ You are strong, you are capable, and you are resilient.

Each challenge is a chance to prove to yourself just how strong you truly are. Rise to the occasion, learn from the experience, and let it shape you into the amazing individual you are meant to be.

This is your space to write, draw, doodle, or sketch your ideas and plans!

10 Tips for Overcoming Challenges

1. **Embrace Challenges:** View challenges not as obstacles but as opportunities for growth and learning.

2. **Believe in Yourself:** You have all the strength and resilience you need within you. Remember that you are capable, smart, and strong.

3. **Find Your Support System:** Surround yourself with positive, supportive individuals - friends, family, mentors - who can provide guidance and encouragement when times get tough.

4. **Learn from Role Models:** Look to the stories of black women who have faced and overcome their own challenges. These can be historical figures, entertainers, athletes, scholars, and more.

5. **Use Affirmations:** Positive affirmations can help boost your self-confidence and reinforce your belief in your ability to overcome challenges.

6. **Develop Problem-Solving Skills:** Challenges often require us to think critically and come up with solutions. Building these skills can make you feel more prepared and confident in facing challenges.

7. **Practice Self-Care:** Physical, emotional, and mental health are key in maintaining the strength and resilience needed to tackle challenges. Make sure to eat healthily, exercise regularly, and take time for relaxation and fun.

8. **Embrace Failure as a Learning Opportunity:** It's okay to stumble or fall. What's important is that you get back up and learn from the experience.

9. **Celebrate Your Achievements:** Small wins are still wins. Celebrate every challenge you overcome, no matter how small it may seem. This can boost your morale and motivate you to tackle bigger challenges.

10. **Keep Moving Forward:** The path to overcoming challenges is rarely a straight line. It's okay to take detours, and it's okay to move at your own pace. What matters most is that you keep moving forward.

Remember, my young queens, that challenges are a natural part of life's journey. They don't exist to break you but to mold you into the incredible individual you are destined to be.

Stand tall, believe in your power, and always keep moving forward. You got this!

Concluding the Chapter on Resilience and Perseverance

As we conclude this chapter, my young queens, remember that your journey is a unique one, filled with both challenges and triumphs.

It's important to understand that obstacles and adversity are not roadblocks but bridges to a stronger, wiser, more resilient you.

Affirmations:

Here are three affirmations to keep in your heart as you navigate your journey:

1. "I am resilient, strong, and capable of overcoming any challenges."
2. "Challenges shape me, but they do not define me."
3. "Every adversity is an opportunity for growth and learning."

 Now, let's draw upon the wisdom of influential black women who have navigated their own paths of resilience and perseverance.

Maya Angelou, a phenomenal poet, memoirist, and civil rights activist, once said,

❞ "You may encounter many defeats, but you must not be defeated. In fact, it may be necessary to encounter the defeats, so you can know who you are, what you can rise from, how you can still come out of it."

Similarly, First Lady, Michelle Obama, a lawyer, author, and former First Lady of the United States, reminds us,

- "You should never view your challenges as a disadvantage. Instead, it's important for you to understand that your experience facing and overcoming adversity is actually one of your biggest advantages."

- And let's not forget the powerful words of actress and singer Ethel Waters, "We are all gifted. That is our inheritance."

So, my young queens, as you move forward, remember the strength and resilience you carry within you.

Remember that no challenge is too great, and you have the power to overcome and rise above. Carry these lessons with you, hold your head high, and continue to shine brilliantly as the queens you are.

CHAPTER: 4

Relationships and Communication

> "What I want young women and girls to know is: You are powerful and your voice matters."
>
> - Vice President Kamala Harris

Relationships and Communication

As you journey through life, the connections you build and the ways you communicate become critical facets of your personal growth and development.

> In this chapter, we explore the importance of nurturing healthy relationships and effective communication.

Relationships can serve as mirrors, reflecting back to us what we need to understand about ourselves.

- They can provide comfort, guidance, challenge, and inspiration.
- They can teach us about trust, empathy, patience, and love.

And communication within these relationships allows us to express our thoughts and feelings, to assert our boundaries, and to deepen our connections with others. The ability to express yourself with clarity and confidence, to listen to others with an open heart and mind, and to navigate the complexities of relationships are all vital skills.

> As a growing queen, mastering these will not only strengthen your interpersonal relationships but also your relationship with yourself.

Chapter Overview:

Here's an overview of what we'll explore in this chapter:

1. **Building Healthy Relationships:** We will delve into what makes a relationship healthy and how to cultivate and maintain these relationships in your life.

2. **Asserting Your Boundaries:** We will learn about the importance of setting and respecting boundaries in relationships and how to do so effectively.

3. **The Art of Communication:** We will explore the various elements of effective communication, including expressing oneself, active listening, and managing conflicts.

Affirmations:

Here are some affirmations to guide us through this journey:

1. "I attract healthy and positive relationships in my life."

2. "My voice is valuable, and I express my feelings and thoughts with clarity and respect."

3. "I set and maintain boundaries to protect my peace and well-being."

And as media mogul Oprah Winfrey reminds us, "Surround yourself only with people who are going to lift you higher."

And always remember, every relationship you form should be a reflection of the respect and love you hold for yourself. Let's dive into this critical journey of understanding relationships and communication.

BUILDING HEALTHY RELATIONSHIPS

❋ Relationships are like gardens; they need attention, care, and nurturing to thrive.

Healthy relationships encourage us to be our best selves, providing a safe space for love, understanding, growth, and mutual respect.

A healthy relationship, whether it's with friends, family, or later in life with a partner, brings joy, provides support, and enriches our lives.

> **The foundation of a healthy relationship lies in respect, trust, honesty, good communication, and understanding. But, also remember that it's perfectly okay to grow apart from people and that you should always prioritize your well-being in any relationship.**

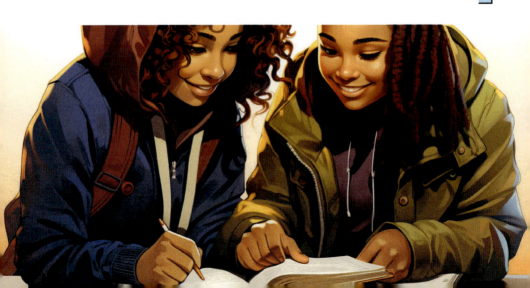

AFFIRMATIONS:

Here are some affirmations to remember as you navigate your relationships:

1. "I surround myself with people who respect and appreciate me for who I am."
2. "I am worthy of relationships that bring joy, love, and positivity into my life."
3. "I attract friends who encourage and support my dreams and growth."

REFLECTIVE QUESTIONS:

Reflect on these affirmations with the following questions:

1. Think about your closest friends. How do they show you respect and understanding?
2. What qualities do you value most in a friend, and why?
3. Can you recall a situation when a friend stood by your side during a difficult time? How did it make you feel?

❗❗ Remember, as tennis superstar Serena Williams puts it, "I surround myself with positive, productive people of goodwill and decency." You, too, should prioritize relationships that value you, respect you, and bring out the best in you.

This is your space to write, draw, doodle, or sketch your ideas and plans!

Expressing Yourself Effectively

> Communication is a powerful tool. It allows us to share our thoughts, express our feelings, and connect with others.

One of the essential parts of communication is the ability to express yourself effectively.

* This means being able to articulate your thoughts, feelings, and needs clearly and respectfully.

Expressing yourself effectively helps in building trust and understanding in your relationships It encourages open dialogue, prevents misunderstandings, and empowers you to stand up for what you believe in.

AFFIRMATIONS:

Here are some affirmations to help you nurture this skill:

1. "My thoughts and feelings are valid, and I express them confidently."
2. "I communicate my needs and boundaries respectfully and clearly."
3. "I have the courage to speak my truth, even if my voice shakes."

REFLECTIVE QUESTIONS:

Reflect on these affirmations with the following questions:

1. Think about a time when you found it hard to express your feelings. What held you back, and how can you overcome it next time?
2. How can you ensure that you express your thoughts and feelings respectfully?
3. How do you feel when you're able to express yourself clearly and effectively?

 Always remember the inspiring words of civil rights activist Fannie Lou Hamer, "I am sick and tired of being sick and tired."

Hamer used her voice to fight for what she believed in, no matter how difficult the journey was. You, too, have a voice. It's powerful, and it deserves to be heard.

This is your space to write, draw, doodle, or sketch your ideas and plans!

NAVIGATING CONFLICTS

Conflicts can be challenging, but they are a natural part of relationships and personal growth.

* How we handle these disagreements can significantly influence our connections with others and the resolution of the issues at hand.

> It's essential to approach conflicts with patience, understanding, and respect, turning these moments into opportunities for learning and growth rather than sources of division.

Remember, it's okay to disagree, but it's not okay to disrespect. Listening to understand, expressing your feelings without blame, and seeking solutions rather than arguments are keys to navigating conflicts effectively.

AFFIRMATIONS:

Here are some affirmations to guide you during challenging times:

1. "I approach conflicts with patience and understanding, seeking resolution over argument."

2. "Even when I disagree, I respect the feelings and perspectives of others."

3. "I express my feelings in conflicts clearly and respectfully, seeking understanding over being right."

REFLECTIVE QUESTIONS:

Reflect on these affirmations with the following questions:

1. Recall a recent conflict you had. How did you handle it? Is there anything you wish you had done differently?

2. How can you ensure that you're listening to understand, not just to reply, during a disagreement?

3. What strategies can you use to express your feelings during a conflict without resorting to blame or disrespect?

❥❥ Remember, as the renowned author and poet Nikki Giovanni said, "The ability to respect the outsider is probably the litmus test of true seeing. And it's damn hard."

But no matter how hard it may seem, you have the power to navigate conflicts with grace, empathy, and understanding, leading to stronger relationships and a deeper understanding of others and yourself.

This is your space to write, draw, doodle, or sketch your ideas and plans!

The Impact of Social Media on Socialization and Communication

In the age of technology, social media has become a significant part of our lives, shaping how we interact, communicate, and perceive the world around us.

For you, as middle school girls, social media can be a powerful tool, connecting you with peers, exposing you to diverse ideas, and offering a platform for self-expression.

> **However, it's crucial to remember that social media also brings certain challenges, especially when it comes to socialization and communication.**

Unlike face-to-face interactions, communication on social media often lacks essential elements such as tone of voice, facial expressions, and body language.

❋ These non-verbal cues are crucial for understanding others' feelings and intentions. Without them, messages can easily be misinterpreted, leading to miscommunication and potential conflict.

Social media can also amplify feelings of alienation or exclusion. The pressure to maintain a 'perfect' image online, the desire for likes, shares, positive comments, and the fear of missing out can lead to feelings of inadequacy and isolation.

> **The highlight reels we see on our feeds rarely represent the whole reality of people's lives, but it's easy to forget that when you're scrolling through perfectly curated posts.**

Sadly, the relative anonymity of social media can also give rise to harmful behaviors like cyberbullying. Harmful comments that might never be said in person can be typed out behind the safety of a screen, causing profound hurt and distress.

So, how can we navigate these challenges? Here are a few pointers:

1. **Digital Literacy:** Learn to differentiate between people's online personas and their real lives. Remember that what you see on social media is often a carefully selected presentation, not the full picture.

2. **Empathy and Respect:** Treat others online as you would want to be treated in person. Remember that behind every profile is a real person with feelings just like yours.

3. **Critical Thinking:** Don't believe everything you see or read online. Check the facts, question the source, and think critically about the information you consume.

4. **Boundaries:** It's okay to take breaks from social media. Prioritize your mental health and well-being. You don't need to be constantly connected.

5. **Speak Up:** If you witness or experience bullying or any inappropriate behavior online, don't hesitate to report it and talk to a trusted adult about it.

Remember, technology and social media are tools. Like any tool, their impact depends on how we use them.

> As the pioneering astronaut Mae Jemison said, "It's your place in the world; it's your life. Go on and do all you can with it, and make it the life you want to live."

This includes your digital life. With careful use and a thoughtful approach, you can make your social media experience positive, enriching, and empowering.

Chapter Conclusion: Relationships and Communication

As we close this chapter, let's remember the critical role relationships and communication play in our lives. These interactions help shape our identities, mold our experiences, and play a big part in our happiness and overall well-being.

Let's take a moment to reflect on the wise words of Beyoncé, a powerhouse in the entertainment industry, an advocate for equality, and a role model for many young girls around the world.

❗❗ She once said, "You determine your self-worth. You don't have to depend on someone telling you who you are."

> **This profound insight applies as much to your relationships as to your self-perception.**

You have the power to shape your relationships and interactions, online and offline. Remember to approach each conversation and connection with respect, empathy, and understanding. As Issa Rae, creator, and star of the show 'Insecure,' beautifully put it, "I thrive on obstacles. If I'm told that it can't be done, then I push harder."

 Use the challenges that come your way as stepping stones to greater strength, wisdom, and resilience.

Affirmations:

In the spirit of these strong women, here are some closing affirmations from this chapter:

1. "I have the power to build healthy, enriching relationships."
2. "My voice is valid and deserves to be heard. I express myself confidently and respectfully."
3. "I navigate conflicts with empathy and understanding, always seeking growth and resolution."

As you turn the page to the next chapter, carry these insights and affirmations with you. May they guide you in your journey of self-discovery and growth, helping you foster meaningful, positive connections along the way.

This is your space to write, draw, doodle, or sketch your ideas and plans!

Chapter: 5

Ambition and Achievement

> "I love you. You are beautiful. You can do anything."
>
> - Lizzo

AMBITION AND ACHIEVEMENT

There is a fire that burns within each one of us. This fire, your ambition, is the spark that ignites your dreams and drives your journey toward achievement.

Ambition is about more than just setting goals; it's about having the determination and drive to reach for those stars and never settling for less than you deserve.

> In this chapter, we will explore what it means to be ambitious and how that ambition can fuel your success.

Through the wisdom shared by our forebearers and current trailblazers, we aim to inspire you, our young queens, to dream big, work hard, and, most importantly, believe in your potential to achieve greatness.

 To quote the first African-American woman astronaut, Mae Jemison, "Never be limited by other people's limited imaginations."

This chapter is about breaking free of any boundaries that might restrict your dreams and daring to imagine a future without limits.

As you journey through this chapter, you will discover the value of ambition, the power of resilience in achieving your goals, and the importance of celebrating your achievements—big and small.

> The affirmations and reflections here will guide you in forging a path marked by determination, perseverance, and success.

Key Takeaways:

Key takeaways from this chapter include:

1. **The Power of Ambition:** Embrace your dreams and aspirations, and let them guide your actions and decisions.

2. **Resilience in the face of obstacles:** Obstacles are a part of every journey towards achievement. Embrace them as opportunities for growth and learning.

3. **Celebrating Your Achievements:** Every achievement, big or small, is a testament to your hard work and determination. Celebrate them all!

Remember, young queens, you hold the power to achieve greatness. As Serena Williams, a tennis superstar and an embodiment of ambition and achievement, once said,

> "The success of every woman should be the inspiration to another. We should raise each other up."

This chapter is about raising you up, inspiring you to embrace your ambition, and propel yourself towards achievement. Let's embark on this journey together.

Setting Goals

Goals are the stepping stones on the path to your dreams. They give you a clear direction and purpose, turning your ambitions into achievable targets.

Goals are powerful because they require you to envision your future, and in doing so, you start to create the blueprint for your success.

Let's take inspiration from Oprah Winfrey, a titan of media and philanthropy, who once said,

> "Create the highest, grandest vision possible for your life because you become what you believe."

> **Your goals are the first tangible representations of this vision. Remember, your goals should be personal and meaningful to you.**

It's not about what others expect but what you want for yourself. They should challenge you but also be attainable with hard work and perseverance.

Affirmations:

Here are some affirmations to help you in setting your goals:

1. "I am capable of achieving any goal I set for myself."

2. "My goals are a reflection of my potential and ambition."

3. "I embrace challenges because they are opportunities for growth."

Reflective Questions:

As you reflect on your goals, consider the following questions:

1. What is one goal you want to achieve in the next year? This could be academic, personal, or related to an extracurricular activity.

2. Why is this goal important to you? Understanding why a goal matters to you can help you stay motivated when challenges arise.

3. What steps will you take to achieve this goal? Breaking down your goal into smaller steps can make it feel more manageable and give you a clear plan for achieving it.

❝ In the words of successful entrepreneur Janice Bryant Howroyd, "Don't just lean in, step up, and step forward."

Setting goals is your first step forward toward the grand vision you have for your life. Embrace this journey with an open mind and a determined heart.

This is your space to write, draw, doodle, or sketch your ideas and plans!

Pursuing Dreams

> Dreams are the whispers of your soul, echoing your deepest desires and ambitions. They are the seeds from which your potential can bloom into beautiful realities.

In pursuing your dreams, you claim ownership of your future and commit to a path of self-fulfillment and achievement.

❗❗ "The most common way people give up their power is by thinking they don't have any."
-Alice Walker

By pursuing your dreams, you not only shape your own life but also become an inspiration for others.

- Remember, the pursuit of dreams is not always a straight path.
- It is often filled with twists, turns, and hurdles.
- But these are not indicators of failure; rather, they are opportunities for growth and learning.

Affirmations:

Here are some affirmations to guide you as you pursue your dreams:

1. "My dreams are valid and worthy of pursuit."
2. "I have the strength and determination to follow my dreams, no matter the challenges."
3. "Every step I take brings me closer to my dreams."

Reflective Questions:

As you reflect on your dreams, consider the following questions:

1. What is a dream you are passionate about? This could be a career aspiration, a personal goal, or an experience you'd like to have.
2. What motivates you to pursue this dream? Understanding your "why" can fuel your motivation during difficult times.
3. Who is a person that inspires you in your pursuit of this dream? This could be a family member, a historical figure, or someone from your community. What qualities do they have that you admire?

❣️ As you embark on the journey to fulfill your dreams, take to heart the words of tennis champion Venus Williams, "You have to believe in yourself when no one else does - that's what makes you a winner."

Believe in yourself, believe in your dreams, and remember, you have all it takes to make them come true.

This is your space to write, draw, doodle, or sketch your ideas and plans!

The Pursuit of Dreams: A Spotlight on Viola Davis

Viola Davis, the award-winning actress and producer, has often spoken about her journey to success, a journey marked by unyielding determination, relentless pursuit of dreams, and a firm belief in her own worth.

Her story is a beacon of inspiration for all of us, particularly for young black girls like you, who are at the dawn of charting their own paths.

> Born in South Carolina, Davis was raised in Rhode Island in a family that struggled with poverty. Despite the challenges she faced, Davis found her passion in acting.

 She would later recall, "I chose acting as a survival mechanism. It was either this or death." Here was a dream born out of a desire for more, a vision of a life filled with opportunities and success.

While her talent was undeniable, Davis found herself battling stereotypes and limited roles for black actresses. But she refused to let these limitations define her or her career.

She persisted, honing her craft and raising her voice against the inequality in the industry. This led to roles that showcased her remarkable talent and finally earned her the recognition she deserved.

❗❗ Reflecting on her journey, Davis once shared, "The only thing that separates women of color from anyone else is opportunity."

She used her platform to advocate for more diverse and complex roles for women of color in Hollywood, creating opportunities not just for herself but for others as well.

Affirmations:

Here are three affirmations inspired by Viola Davis:

1. "I will not let anyone else define my worth or limit my opportunities."
2. "I am resilient, powerful, and capable of achieving my dreams."
3. "I have the strength to challenge norms and create opportunities for myself."

Viola Davis' story is a testament to the power of dreams, the importance of perseverance, and the impact of challenging the status quo. As you pursue your dreams, remember her journey. Remember that your dreams are valid and worthy, and you are capable of overcoming obstacles in your path. Never limit your potential, and never allow anyone else to limit it, either. You are powerful, you are capable, and your dreams are within your reach.

Overcoming Obstacles to Success

Success is a journey, not a destination, and this journey often includes obstacles.

These challenges might seem daunting, but they are actually opportunities for growth and self-discovery. They build character and resilience and provide valuable lessons that empower us to reach greater heights.

Katherine Johnson, the trailblazing mathematician and NASA scientist who played a key role in the success of the US space program, faced numerous obstacles in her path.

From the limitations imposed by segregation to gender bias in the male-dominated field of mathematics, she had her fair share of challenges.

However, she overcame them with her intellect, tenacity, and courage.

> Johnson once said, "I counted everything. I counted the steps to the road, the steps up to the church, the number of dishes and silverware I washed … anything that could be counted, I did." It was this meticulous, unwavering focus that helped her overcome the obstacles she faced.

> Remember, the path to your dreams may not always be smooth, but the trials you face can be used to your advantage. They can mold you into a stronger, more resilient person, ready to conquer anything that stands in your way.

Affirmations:

Here are some affirmations to inspire you as you face and overcome obstacles:

1. "My dreams are valid and worthy of pursuit."
2. "I have the strength and determination to follow my dreams, no matter the challenges."
3. "Every step I take brings me closer to my dreams."

Reflective Questions:

Reflect on these questions:

1. What are some obstacles you have faced in the past, and how have you overcome them? This can help you understand your own resilience and ability to overcome adversity.
2. What is an obstacle you are currently facing, and what strategies can you use to overcome it? This can help you create a plan and focus on solutions rather than problems.
3. How can overcoming this obstacle make you stronger or help you grow? This can help you view obstacles as opportunities rather than setbacks.

❚❚ In the face of adversity, let us remember the words of acclaimed author Zora Neale Hurston, "I will fight for my heart's desire with all my strength."

Your heart's desire is worth fighting for. Be ready to overcome any obstacles that come your way and continue moving towards your dreams.

This is your space to write, draw, doodle, or sketch your ideas and plans!

Chapter Conclusion: Ambition and Achievement

Our journey through this chapter has shown us the power of ambition, the pursuit of dreams, and the importance of overcoming obstacles.

> Each section served as a beacon, illuminating the path towards achievement and the realization of your dreams.

Let us remember the words of celebrated tennis champion Serena Williams, who defied the odds to become one of the greatest athletes of all time:

> "I really think a champion is defined not by their wins but by how they can recover when they fall." Remember, dear queens, stumbling blocks are not the end of the journey; they are stepping stones toward your success.

Affirmations:

Look back on the affirmations we shared in this chapter and remember to hold them close to your heart. Repeat them when you need an extra boost of motivation or when you face challenges:

1. "I am capable of setting goals and achieving them."
2. "I will relentlessly pursue my dreams, no matter what."
3. "I have the resilience to overcome any obstacle on my path to success."

The reflections shared in this chapter are intended to serve as a guide, providing insight and perspective. As you face the challenges of middle school and, indeed life, remember to use these reflections as tools to help you navigate your path.

* It's important to remember that no one's path is completely smooth or free of obstacles.

The narrative of Viola Davis shows us that our dreams are worth fighting for, and the story of Katherine Johnson reinforces that we can overcome any obstacles with determination and focus.

> This chapter's essence lies in its ability to inspire you to dream big, set ambitious goals, and develop the grit to achieve them. It encourages you to view challenges as opportunities for growth and reminds you of your innate ability to overcome them.

❞ Remember, in the words of President Barack Obama, "Focusing your life solely on making a buck shows a certain poverty of ambition. It asks too little of yourself. Because it's only when you hitch your wagon to something larger than yourself that you realize your true potential."

Never underestimate your power, your potential, and the impact you can make. Carry these lessons with you, use them as stepping stones on your journey to achievement, and watch as your ambition transforms your world.

> **You are destined for greatness, dear queens. Believe in it, strive for it, and make it happen.**

This is your space to write, draw, doodle, or sketch your ideas and plans!

Activity: The Challenge Bridge
You can engage in this activity as an individual or group.

* Objective: The purpose of this activity is to help middle school students understand and develop strategies to overcome obstacles that might stand in their way to success.

 Material Needed

- ✓ Journal and pen
- ✓ A large piece of paper and markers (optional)

Instructions:

- Identify the Challenge: Have the students identify a current challenge or obstacle they are facing. It can be anything from a complex subject at school, to a challenging relationship, to an ambitious goal they want to achieve. They should write this at the top of a page in their journal.

- Visualize the Challenge: Have the students draw a river on a piece of paper, with one bank representing where they are now and the other bank representing their goal or the successful resolution of their challenge. The river represents the obstacle they have identified.

- Build the Bridge: In this step, the students should think about the steps or strategies they can use to cross the river.

- They should consider things like persistence, seeking help when needed, breaking their goal into manageable parts, focusing on solutions rather than the problem, and believing in themselves. Have them write these steps as planks on the bridge crossing the river.

- Reflect on the Challenge: Now, students should write a brief reflection in their journal about how they felt while doing this activity. Did it make the challenge seem more manageable? Did it help them come up with a clear plan to overcome the obstacle?

- Review and Repeat: Finally, encourage the students to keep this piece of paper and their journal entry as a reminder of their ability to overcome obstacles. As new challenges arise, they can repeat this activity to help them develop a plan and build their confidence.

By completing this activity, middle school girls can tangibly see that no obstacle is too big to overcome. They'll have a roadmap for success and a tool to use when new challenges arise.

Remember, the ability to overcome obstacles is not a trait that some people are born with - it's a skill that can be learned and improved over time.

Fearless Hearts: A Collection of Fatherly
Affirmations for Young Black Queens

This is your space to write, draw, doodle, or sketch your ideas and plans!

CHAPTER: 6

Body Image and Health

> "I am no longer accepting the things I cannot change. I am changing the things I cannot accept."
>
> - Angela Davis

BODY IMAGE AND HEALTH

Embarking on this chapter, we delve into one of the most important journeys, the journey towards embracing our body image and understanding our health.

> This chapter is about cultivating a positive body image, respecting your body, and understanding the importance of maintaining physical and mental health.

Middle school can often present challenges as you are growing and changing. With influences around you, from peers to media, it can sometimes be difficult always to feel good about yourself.

❈ This chapter provides tools to help navigate these waters and affirm your self-worth and beauty.

We start with the words of the vibrant Solange Knowles, who reminds us,

❝ "I have chosen to no longer be apologetic for my femaleness and my femininity. And I want to be respected in all my femaleness because I deserve to be."

> It's essential for you, our young queens, to understand that your value is not tied to any external validation but to the beautiful person you are inside.

Throughout this chapter, we aim to:

1. Embrace your body: Encourage an understanding that everybody is unique and special in its own way. Your body is a powerful vessel that allows you to experience the world, and it deserves respect and care.

2. Understand health: Understanding that good health is a holistic concept encompassing physical, mental, and emotional well-being.

3. Cultivate self-care habits: Learning to take care of your body and mind, understanding the importance of nutrition, sleep, exercise, and mental health practices.

> Stay with us on this journey as we explore these topics, learn, reflect, and grow together. In the words of the phenomenal actress Lupita Nyong'o, "You can't rely on how you look to sustain you. What is fundamentally beautiful is compassion for yourself and for those around you." As you navigate through this chapter, keep this thought close to your heart.
>
> Now, let's begin.

LOVING YOUR BODY

Welcome to the section on Loving Your Body. In a world where external validation often takes precedence, we must learn to love and accept ourselves just as we are.

The journey of self-love is an ongoing process, one that begins within. Also, loving your body is a powerful act of self-acceptance.

* For middle school black girls, this is a transformative time, a period of discovery and embracing who you are. Understanding that every shape, size, and shade is beautiful is essential in cultivating a positive self-image.

> In this section, we will explore the beauty of self-love, a love that is not determined by societal standards or peer pressures but guided by the unique beauty that you possess.

AFFIRMATIONS:

1. "I am unique, I am beautiful, and my beauty is defined by me and no one else." Remember that beauty comes in all shapes, sizes, and colors. Your skin, your hair, your eyes - every feature of yours is beautiful and unique to you.

2. "I celebrate and honor my body as my home and respect its needs and boundaries." It is vital to listen to your body, respect its needs, and appreciate the incredible things it allows you to do every day.

3. "I am more than my physical appearance. I am a magnificent blend of mind, body, and spirit." You are a complete package, a blend of intellect, compassion, creativity, and courage.

REFLECTIVE QUESTIONS:

Reflect on these affirmations with the following questions:

1. 1. What does self-love mean to you? Is it about accepting yourself, feeling comfortable in your skin, or something else? There is no right or wrong answer.

2. 2. How do you feel about your body? Do you appreciate its functions, its strength, its resilience?

3. 3. What can you do to show your body more love and respect? Are there habits or practices you can adopt, such as exercise, balanced nutrition, or positive self-talk?

This journey of self-love is a personal one. It's all about discovering and embracing the beauty that you hold within and reflecting it on the outside.

As we move forward, remember these affirmations and keep them close to your heart. Loving your body is the first step to empowering yourself.

❞ As the renowned supermodel Naomi Campbell stated, "I am my own work of art."

> **You are your own masterpiece, an embodiment of beauty, strength, and grace. Believe this, cherish this, and most importantly, love this.**

This is your space to write, draw, doodle, or sketch your ideas and plans!

Dealing with Body Changes and Puberty

Puberty is a time of change. As you transition from a child to a teenager, your body goes through a series of changes that are completely natural and normal.

These changes are a part of growing up and becoming the person you're meant to be. During this time, it's crucial to remember that every person's journey is unique and these changes occur at their own pace.

* It's all part of the beautiful diversity of life.

> Remember, no matter the changes you're experiencing, you're growing into a beautiful, unique individual. Embrace this journey of transformation and take care of yourself throughout.

AFFIRMATIONS:

1. "I embrace the changes happening to my body, as they are a natural part of growing up." It's important to remember that everyone experiences these changes, and they are a completely natural part of life.

2. "I am more than my physical appearance. My worth comes from within." Our self-worth is not defined by our physical appearance, but by who we are inside: our values, our kindness, our intellect, and our strength.

3. "I respect my body and will take care of it." Our bodies are our homes. By taking care of our physical health, we take care of our overall well-being.

REFLECTIVE QUESTIONS:

Reflect on these affirmations with the following questions:

1. What feelings or thoughts are you experiencing as your body changes? How can you embrace these changes as a natural part of growing up?

2. How can you remind yourself that your self-worth is not tied to your physical appearance? What qualities do you value about yourself beyond your looks?

3. How can you take care of your body during this time of change? What self-care practices might you implement?

This is your space to write, draw, doodle, or sketch your ideas and plans!

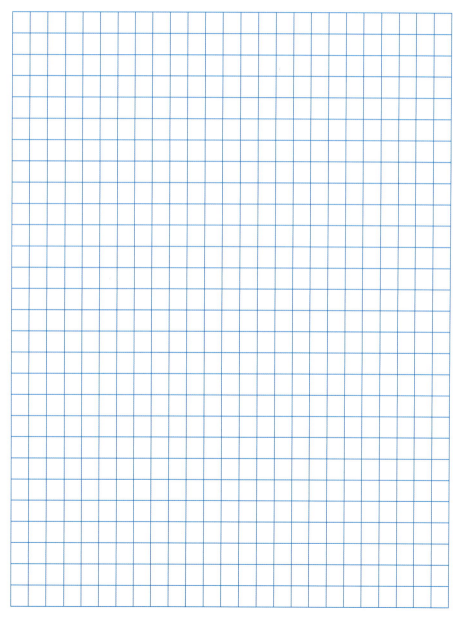

Daily Affirmations for Body Positivity

Body positivity is all about embracing your body as it is, right now. It's about respecting your body's unique features and recognizing its strength and abilities.

It's about rejecting societal pressures to look a certain way and acknowledging that all bodies are good bodies.

- With daily affirmations, you can foster a positive attitude towards your body and help boost your self-confidence.

- By repeating these affirmations regularly, you can create a habit of body positivity.

Embrace your body's uniqueness and strength, and treat it with the care and respect it deserves. Remember, you are enough just as you are.

❋ Your beauty is unparalleled, and your body is a testament to your strength and resilience. Let these affirmations serve as daily reminders of your inherent worth and beauty.

Affirmations:

1. "I am beautiful exactly as I am. My beauty is unique and cannot be compared." Recognize that your beauty is one-of-a-kind and that comparison to others is unhelpful. You are beautiful in your own special way.

2. "I love and appreciate my body. It carries me each day and allows me to experience life." Gratitude towards your body for all it does can help foster a positive mindset.

3. "My body is strong, resilient, and worthy of care and respect." Acknowledge your body's strength and resilience, and the importance of treating it with care and respect.

Reflective Questions:

1. How do you feel when you say these affirmations to yourself? Do you believe them? If not, what might be getting in the way?

2. How can you show your body love and appreciation daily? What are some actions you can take?

3. What does being strong and resilient mean to you? How can you remind yourself of your body's strength and resilience when you're feeling down?

This is your space to write, draw, doodle, or sketch your ideas and plans!

Conclusion: Body Image and Health

We've journeyed together through a very important chapter - one that has focused on loving your body, understanding the changes it goes through, and prioritizing your health and fitness.

Throughout this journey, I hope you've begun to realize just how incredible your body truly is. It's not just about how it looks, but about all the amazing things it can do.

❝❝ In the words of global superstar Lizzo, "I love you. You are beautiful. You can do anything."

> Remember this as an affirmation of self-love and self-acceptance, no matter how your body looks or changes. Your body is yours, and it is beautiful.

Affirmations:

🌸 Affirmation: "I love my body. I am grateful for everything it does for me."

Your body is also your lifelong companion, so taking care of it should be one of your top priorities. Serena Williams, a phenomenal athlete, showed us the importance of health and fitness, not just to win games, but to thrive in life.

🌸 Affirmation: "I honor my body by making healthy choices and staying active."

Navigating puberty can be challenging, but remember that it's a natural part of growing up. It's not something to fear or feel embarrassed about. As actress and activist Yara Shahidi once stated, "My blackness does not inhibit me from being beautiful and intelligent. In fact, it is the reason I am beautiful and intelligent." Embrace the changes, and don't let them inhibit you from recognizing your beauty and worth.

🌸 Affirmation: "I embrace the changes in my body with understanding and patience. These changes are a part of my journey to becoming a young woman."

To conclude, always remember that you are more than just a physical appearance. You are a queen - strong, beautiful, intelligent, and capable of achieving anything you set your mind to. Celebrate your body, nurture your health, and continue on your journey with grace, resilience, and self-love.

> **The world is waiting for you, beautiful queen. Go out and conquer it, one healthy and positive step at a time.**

This is your space to write, draw, doodle, or sketch your ideas and plans!

CHAPTER: 7

Empowerment and Leadership

"I am my own work of art."

- Naomi Campbell

Empowerment and Leadership

> The time has come for you to tap into your innate power. Empowerment and leadership are more than just words; they are pillars of strength and catalysts for change.

This chapter is designed to affirm your potential, illuminate your path to empowerment, and fuel your journey towards becoming a leader in your own right.

❞ As former First Lady, First Lady, Michelle Obama, affirms, "There is no limit to what we, as women, can accomplish." These are not just words.

They are the essence of empowerment and leadership. Leadership is not only about leading others. It's about leading your life with integrity, respect, and the courage to make the right choices, even when those choices are difficult.

 Empowerment is about acknowledging your worth, owning your space, and using your voice for good.

Key Takeaways:

1. Empowerment is personal: Your empowerment comes from within, it's about believing in your worth, and your ability to make a difference.

2. Leadership is inclusive: A good leader listens, understands, and values the perspectives of others. Leadership is about uniting and guiding, not dividing and commanding.

3. Every voice matters: Your voice, your ideas, your experiences, and your dreams are important. Don't be afraid to share them.

The journey to empowerment and leadership is yours to undertake. It will challenge you, it will change you, and most importantly, it will empower you.

❕❕ Remember the words of poet Audre Lorde, "I am my best work - a series of road maps, reports, recipes, doodles, and prayers from the front lines."

As you navigate through this chapter, remember that you are your best work. You are empowered. You are a leader.

Becoming a Leader

Leadership is not defined by age, but by actions. It begins with taking responsibility, making informed decisions, and guiding others along the way.

Embracing leadership is about standing up and being a positive influence, no matter how small or large the situation.

> As you reflect on these affirmations and questions, envision yourself as the leader you aim to be. You have the power to make a positive impact, to lead, and inspire those around you.

AFFIRMATIONS:

1. "I am a leader. I inspire others with my words and actions." Remember, leadership isn't about being the loudest voice in the room; it's about inspiring others with your actions and words.

2. "I am confident and capable. I can make wise decisions." Confidence is key in leadership. Believe in your ability to make informed decisions. Remember, it's okay to seek advice and listen to the opinions of others.

3. "I respect and value others' perspectives. I create an environment of unity and understanding." A great leader listens and respects the views of others. When we encourage an environment of understanding, we build stronger teams and relationships.

REFLECTIVE QUESTIONS:

Reflect on these affirmations with the following questions:

1. Can you remember a time when you naturally took on a leadership role? What did you learn from this experience?

2. What qualities do you admire in leaders around you? How can you incorporate these traits into your own style of leadership?

3. Leadership comes with challenges. What challenges do you anticipate facing as a leader, and how might you handle them?

This is your space to write, draw, doodle, or sketch your ideas and plans!

Influencing Others Positively

In our journey towards becoming the best version of ourselves, we often forget the power we hold to positively influence those around us.

Just as you are a queen, there are many other young queens out there who might need a bit of encouragement, guidance, and positivity in their lives.

Remember that by being a beacon of positivity, you're not just illuminating your path, but also lighting the way for others.

> Beyoncé, one of the world's most influential women, once said, "Your self-worth is determined by you. You don't have to depend on someone telling you who you are."

By choosing to be a positive influence, you're embracing your self-worth and empowering others to do the same.

You have the power to create a ripple of positivity around you, and that starts with your words, your actions, and your belief in yourself and others.

AFFIRMATIONS:

1. Affirmation 1: "I am a positive influence in the lives of those around me."
2. Affirmation 2: "My words and actions inspire and uplift others."
3. Affirmation 3: "I am an agent of change, creating a ripple of positivity around me."

REFLECTIVE QUESTIONS:

Reflect on these affirmations with the following questions:

1. Reflection Question 1: Think of a time when someone positively influenced your life. How did their actions or words make a difference? How can you do the same for someone else?
2. Reflection Question 2: Words hold power. What are some positive, encouraging words you can share with your peers today? How can you use your actions to inspire them?
3. Reflection Question 3: Consider a situation in your school or community where you can create a positive change. What steps can you take towards making this change?

 Keep shining your light, young queen. The world needs your positivity and influence.

This is your space to write, draw, doodle, or sketch your ideas and plans!

The Unstoppable Journey of Rihanna

In the grand tapestry of black excellence, there's a thread that shines brilliantly, connecting the Caribbean to the global stage.

This thread, unyielding and iridescent, is none other than Robyn Rihanna Fenty, known to the world as Rihanna. Her story is a testament to the power of ambition and the unyielding spirit of a black girl who refused to be limited by anything or anyone.

Born and raised in Barbados, Rihanna's life was not always filled with glitz and glamour. Growing up, she helped her father sell clothes in a street stall, and lived through her parents' turbulent marriage.

But it was in this environment that Rihanna discovered her passion for music and began to dream of a life beyond her island home.

Armed with her enchanting voice and a heart full of dreams, Rihanna won a school talent show at the age of 15. The following year, she auditioned for acclaimed record producer Evan Rogers, who was vacationing in Barbados.

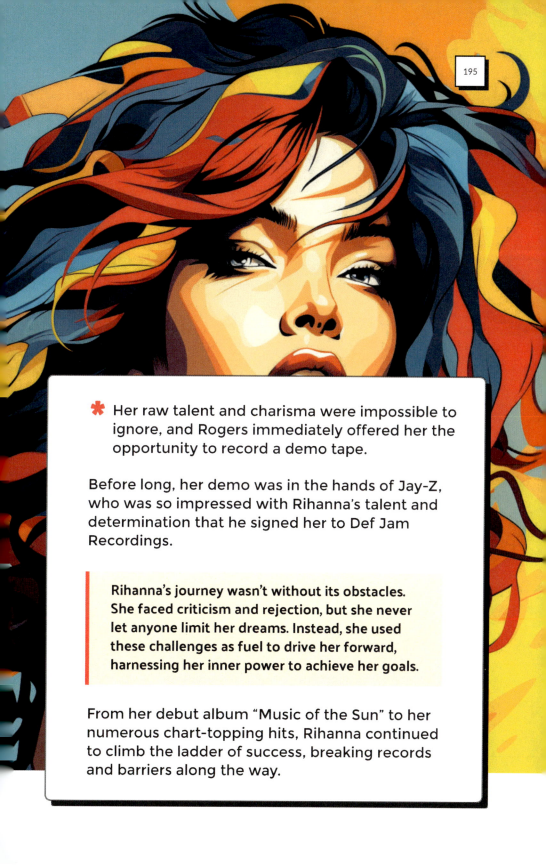

* Her raw talent and charisma were impossible to ignore, and Rogers immediately offered her the opportunity to record a demo tape.

Before long, her demo was in the hands of Jay-Z, who was so impressed with Rihanna's talent and determination that he signed her to Def Jam Recordings.

> Rihanna's journey wasn't without its obstacles. She faced criticism and rejection, but she never let anyone limit her dreams. Instead, she used these challenges as fuel to drive her forward, harnessing her inner power to achieve her goals.

From her debut album "Music of the Sun" to her numerous chart-topping hits, Rihanna continued to climb the ladder of success, breaking records and barriers along the way.

- ✱ But Rihanna didn't stop there. Recognizing the power of her influence, she ventured into the world of beauty and fashion, launching her own inclusive beauty brand, Fenty Beauty, and later, her own luxury fashion house, Fenty, under LVMH.

With these ventures, Rihanna challenged beauty standards and championed diversity, becoming a voice for black girls and women around the world.

- Rihanna's journey teaches us the importance of following our dreams, regardless of where we come from or what obstacles stand in our way.
- Through her life, we see the unlimited power and potential that lies within each and every one of us. Her story tells us that we, as black girls, can rise above any challenges, break through any barriers, and achieve whatever goals we set our hearts on.

So, my dear queens, let Rihanna's journey inspire you. Dream big, aim high, and don't let anyone limit your opportunities, your brilliance, your power, your purpose, your desires, or your goals.

> **Because within you lies a boundless potential that is just waiting to be unleashed. Remember, you are not just a dreamer, but a doer, a trailblazer, a queen, just like Rihanna.**

Empowering Others

Being a young queen, you hold immense power - not just over your own life, but also in your ability to empower others.

True leadership is about lifting others up, helping them recognize their potential, and encouraging them to reach their goals.

❞ Oprah Winfrey, a titan of empowerment and influence, has said, "The more you celebrate your life, the more there is in life to celebrate."

> By choosing to empower others, you're not just strengthening your community, you're also inviting more celebration and positivity into your own life.

You have the power to ignite a spark of ambition, resilience, and joy in others - and that starts with choosing to be an empowering force in their lives.

AFFIRMATIONS:

1. Affirmation 1: "I am a source of inspiration and empowerment for my peers."
2. Affirmation 2: "I support and uplift others in their journey to success."
3. Affirmation 3: "I celebrate the successes and achievements of others, as their victories are victories for all of us."

REFLECTIVE QUESTIONS:

Reflect on these affirmations with the following questions:

1. Reflection Question 1: How can you use your strengths and achievements to inspire and empower those around you? List three ways you can make a positive impact on others this week.
2. Reflection Question 2: Can you recall a time when you felt supported and uplifted by someone else? How did that make you feel, and how can you provide the same support to others in their times of need?
3. Reflection Question 3: Who in your life can you celebrate today? What achievements have they accomplished that you can acknowledge and applaud?

 Stay strong and keep inspiring, young queen. Your empowerment can change the world.

Fearless Hearts: A Collection of Fatherly Affirmations for Young Black Queens

This is your space to write, draw, doodle, or sketch your ideas and plans!

Daily Affirmations for Leadership

Leadership starts from within, young queens. It is about how you guide yourself in your daily life, how you handle challenges, and how you inspire others by your actions.

❝ Taking inspiration from Vice President Kamala Harris, the first black and Asian-American woman to hold the position, remember, "What I want young women and girls to know is: You are powerful and your voice matters."

As young, vibrant, black queens, your potential for leadership is limitless.

AFFIRMATIONS:

1. Affirmation 1: "I am a capable and confident leader, ready to make positive changes in my world."

2. Affirmation 2: "I have the power to influence others in a positive way, and I choose to use it for the betterment of my community."

3. Affirmation 3: "I face challenges with courage and resilience, knowing that every obstacle is a stepping stone towards growth."

REFLECTIVE QUESTIONS:

Reflect on these affirmations with the following questions:

1. Reflection Question 1: What is one situation today where you can apply your leadership? How will you go about it?

2. Reflection Question 2: Think about someone who positively influences you. What qualities do they possess that you admire? How can you embody these qualities in your own leadership?

3. Reflection Question 3: Recall a challenge you recently faced. How did you handle it? If you encounter a similar challenge in the future, how can you apply your leadership skills to approach it?

Believe in yourself, affirm your strengths, and step into your power every day.

This is your space to write, draw, doodle, or sketch your ideas and plans!

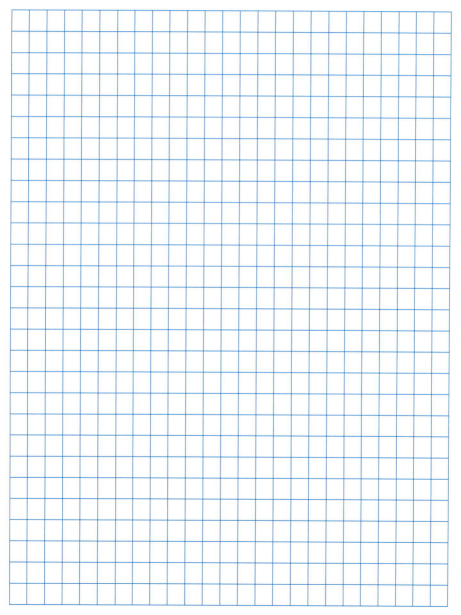

Conclusion: Empowerment and Leadership

This chapter has been an exciting journey into the realm of leadership and empowerment. We've explored:

- what it means to step into leadership roles,
- to use our voices,
- and to stand up for what we believe in.

And remember, as a young black queen, your voice is not just valid, it's vital. You bring to the table a unique perspective that the world needs.

❗❗ The incomparable Beyoncé once said, "Power's not given to you. You have to take it."

That's precisely what empowerment and leadership are all about. They are about recognizing your innate power and taking action to make a positive impact. I want you to remember something special - You are an extraordinary being, capable of changing the world.

> You have inside of you a light that can illuminate the darkest corners. Leadership and empowerment are about letting that light shine for all to see.

Affirmations:

> Here's a challenge for you: each day, try to do something that scares you. Take up space. Raise your voice. Stand up for something you believe in. The world needs you.

❋ Affirmation: "I am a leader. I have the power to effect change, and I use my voice with confidence and courage."

And remember, leadership isn't just about being in charge - it's about taking care of those in your charge. It's about compassion, understanding, and empathy.

❞ First Lady, Michelle Obama captured this beautifully when she said, "Success isn't about how much money you make, it's about the difference you make in people's lives."

❋ Affirmation: "I am a caring leader. I am dedicated to making a positive impact on the lives of others."

As you move through your journey, remember these words and the many lessons in this chapter. You have everything you need inside of you to be an empowered leader.

So, go out there and shine, young queen. The world awaits you.

Fearless Hearts: A Collection of Fatherly Affirmations for Young Black Queens

This is your space to write, draw, doodle, or sketch your ideas and plans!

Ongoing Journey: Continuing the Practice of Affirmations

As we come to the end of this journal, it is essential to remember that your journey of self-discovery, empowerment, and growth does not end here.

> Think of these pages as the first few chapters of a story that is still being written - your story.

Just as each affirmation in this journal has guided you to recognize your worth, build confidence, resilience, develop healthy relationships, pursue your dreams, love your body, and lead with grace, it's up to you to keep this practice going in your everyday life.

Affirmations are more than just words.

- They are personal statements of belief, power, and love.
- They shape our thoughts, influence our attitudes, and guide our actions.
- ✱ The more we repeat them, the stronger their impact becomes, empowering us to reach our full potential and face life's challenges head-on.

AFFIRMATIONS:

1. Affirmative 1: "I am the author of my own story. Each day, I choose to write a new page filled with love, resilience, and courage."

2. Affirmative 2: "My voice matters. I will use it to speak my truth, stand up for myself, and inspire those around me."

3. Affirmative 3: "I am beautiful, inside and out. My uniqueness is my strength, and I will celebrate it every day."

REFLECTIVE QUESTIONS:

As you move forward, create your own affirmations. Let them reflect your dreams, your struggles, your victories, and your hopes. Use them to nurture the queen within you.

1. Reflection Question 1: What is one affirmation you can create that reflects your personal goals?

2. Reflection Question 2: How can you remind yourself to practice affirmations daily?

3. Reflection Question 3: How have these affirmations impacted your perception of yourself and your potential?

The journey to self-love, self-discovery, and empowerment is an ongoing one. It won't always be easy, and there will be days when doubt may creep in.

* In those moments, look back at this journal, remember the affirmations you've penned and embraced, and draw strength from them.

Remember, you are a queen - unique, strong, resilient, and worthy. Always keep these affirmations at the core of your being, for they are the fuel that ignites the limitless potential within you.

> Your journey is ongoing, and each day presents a new opportunity to affirm your worth, strengthen your spirit, and celebrate the incredible young woman you are becoming.

Onwards, our beautiful queens.
Your journey continues, and we are here,
cheering you on every step of the way.

A Father's Hope: Closing Words from Contributors

As we bring this journey of affirmation to a close, we, the contributors of "Fearless Hearts," fathers from different walks of life, want to share our hope for you, our young Black queens.

In every affirmation, piece of wisdom, and advice contained within these pages, we wish to imprint upon your heart one crucial message: You matter, and you are loved.

We understand the power of a father's presence. A father serves as an anchor, a guidepost, and a refuge. His words can provide assurance, build resilience, and inspire ambition.

A father's voice can echo in your mind in times of doubt, reminding you of your worth, your potential, and your ability to rise above any adversity.

However, we also recognize that life doesn't always grant us the perfect circumstances. There may be situations where a father's voice is absent - due to physical distance, the breakdown of relationships, or the painful sting of loss. In these instances, we want to reassure you that there is still a world of guidance and support available to you.

This book, in many ways, is a testament to that. While we may be your fathers in spirit, through these pages, we hope to provide the affirmations you need to navigate your world. Even if the voice you seek to hear is not physically there, the essence of their love and hope for you can be found here.

When a father's voice can't reach, the affirming words of a mentor, a teacher, an uncle, a brother, or even a friend, can step in to fill that gap. They can serve as your cheerleaders, your guides, your protectors, and sometimes, the tough love you might need.

Remember, it's not about who delivers the message, but the message itself. Words of love, support, and affirmation can come from many sources, and they are all equally valuable.

We believe that every young Black girl needs to hear, understand, and believe in their worth. We trust that this journal has provided an opportunity for you to see the love and hope we have for you.

As fathers and mentors, our deepest wish is for you to grow into the powerful, resilient, and vibrant young women we know you can be. We see your strength, your brilliance, and your potential. Always remember that you are our queens, and you are destined for greatness.

Keep these affirmations close to your heart, let them guide you on your journey, and never forget that you are a fearless heart, a young Black queen. Your story is just beginning, and we can't wait to see how it unfolds.

With all our love and hope,
The Fatherly Voices of Fearless Hearts

Made in the USA
Columbia, SC
06 May 2024

6a827b63-fc55-4823-bc34-1ce4d56c28ceR01